SENT

Leader Guide

SENT
Delivering the Gift of Hope at Christmas

Book
978-1-501-80103-7
978-1-501-80104-4 eBook

Devotions for the Season
978-1-501-80117-4
978-1-501-80118-1 eBook

DVD
978-1-501-80108-2

Leader Guide
978-1-501-80106-8
978-1-501-80107-5 eBook

Youth Study Book
978-1-501-80114-3
978-1-501-80115-0 eBook

Children's Leader Guide
978-1-501-80116-7

For more information, visit www.AbingdonPress.com

SENT

DELIVERING
THE GIFT OF HOPE
AT CHRISTMAS

JORGE ACEVEDO
with Jacob Armstrong, Rachel Billups, Justin LaRosa & Lanecia Rouse

Leader Guide
by Martha Bettis Gee

Abingdon Press
Nashville

Sent: Leader Guide
Delivering the Gift of Hope at Christmas

Leader Guide
by Martha Bettis Gee

Copyright © 2015 by Abingdon Press
All rights reserved.

This book is printed on elemental chlorine-free paper.

ISBN 978-1-5018-0106-8

15 16 17 18 19 20 21 22 23 24—10 9 8 7 6 5 4 3 2 1
MANUFACTURED IN THE UNITED STATES OF AMERICA

CONTENTS

TO THE LEADER

Welcome! In this study, you have the opportunity to help a group of learners as they journey through Advent in *Sent: Delivering the Gift of Hope at Christmas*. As noted by Jorge Acevedo, the study's principal author, the early church fathers and mothers had the great wisdom to set aside the four weeks leading up to Christmas as a time to prepare for the birth of Jesus Christ. The word *advent* means "arrival" or "coming." The birth of Jesus was a historical event that took place in a particular time and place, and yet every Christmas has the potential for Jesus to be born anew, in our lives and in the world.

In this study, learners can explore what it means for Christ to be sent by God into our lives and can reflect on how they in turn might be sent into the world as the hands and feet of Christ, not just in this season, but all year long.

Over the course of the study you will hear Advent and Christmas stories of events that changed everything. You will meet Jorge Acevedo and four of his friends and colleagues in ministry—Jacob Armstrong,

Lanecia Rouse, Justin LaRosa, and Rachel Billups. Encountering the stories and perspectives of five different Christians not only provides a depth and diversity beyond the viewpoint of one person; it also encourages participants to explore their own life stories and reflect on the unique lenses they bring to bear on their Christian journey.

Scripture tells us that where two or three are gathered together, we can be assured of the presence of the Holy Spirit, working in and through all those gathered. As you prepare to lead, pray for that presence and expect that you will experience it.

The study includes four sessions for the four weeks of Advent, plus a fifth session for those who would like a session on or after Christmas week. The study makes use of the following components:

- the study book *Sent: Delivering the Gift of Hope at Christmas*, by Jorge Acevedo with Jacob Armstrong, Lanecia Rouse, Justin LaRosa, and Rachel Billups;
- the DVD that accompanies the study;
- this Leader Guide.

Participants in the study will also need Bibles, as well as either a spiral bound notebook for a journal or an electronic means of journaling, such as a tablet. If possible, notify those interested in the study in advance of the first session. Make arrangements for them to get copies of the book so that they can read the Introduction and Chapter 1.

Using This Guide with Your Group

Because no two groups are alike, this guide has been designed to give you flexibility and choice in tailoring the sessions for your group. The session format is listed below. You may choose any or all of the activities, adapting them as you wish to meet the schedule and needs of your particular group.

In many cases your session time will be too short to do all the activities. Select ahead of time which activities the group will do, for how long, and in what order. You will be presented with a variety of activities from which to choose, blending Bible study and study of the material in the study book. Depending on which activities you select, there may be special preparation needed. The leader is alerted in the session plan when advance preparation is needed.

Session Format

Planning the Session

Session Goals
Biblical Foundation
Special Preparation

Getting Started

Opening Activities
Opening Prayer

Learning Together

Video Study and Discussion
Bible and Book Study and Discussion

Wrapping Up

Closing Activities
Closing Prayer

Helpful Hints

Preparing for the Session

- Pray for the leading of the Holy Spirit as you prepare for the study. Pray for discernment for yourself and for each member of the study group.
- Since this is an Advent study, the opening activities suggest the lighting of Advent candles or an Advent wreath, with one additional candle being lit each week of Advent and a final Christ candle lit at the session following Christmas. If your schedule is different, adjust that opening candlelighting ritual.
- Before each session, familiarize yourself with the content. Read the book chapter again.
- Choose the session elements you will use during the group session, including the specific discussion questions you plan to cover. Be prepared, however, to adjust the session as group members interact and as questions arise. Prepare carefully, but allow space for the Holy Spirit to move in and through the group members and through you as facilitator.
- Some sessions suggest the use of online music video clips. If you plan to use them, obtain a video projector for the duration of the study. Adults with smartphones can access the clips in that way, but this is less effective.
- Prepare the room where the group will meet so that the space will enhance the learning process. Ideally, group members should be seated around a table or in a circle so that all can see each other. Movable chairs are best, because the group will often be forming pairs or small groups for discussion.
- Bring a supply of Bibles for those who forget to bring their own. Some sessions use a variety of translations. If you don't have access to different translations, you can find many translations of a particular passage at a website such as BibleGateway.com.

- For most sessions you will also need a chalkboard and chalk, a whiteboard and markers, or an easel with paper and markers.

Shaping the Learning Environment

- Begin and end on time.
- Create a climate of openness, encouraging group members to participate as they feel comfortable. Some participants may find aspects of this study quite challenging. Be on the lookout for signs of discomfort or uncertainty in those who may be silent, and encourage them to express their thoughts and feelings honestly.
- Remember that some people will jump right in with answers and comments, while others need time to process what is being discussed.
- If you notice that some group members seem never to be able to enter the conversation, ask them if they have thoughts to share. Give everyone a chance to talk, but keep the conversation moving. Moderate to prevent a few individuals from doing all the talking.
- Communicate the importance of group discussions and group exercises.
- If no one answers at first during discussions, do not be afraid of silence. Count silently to ten, then say something such as, "Would anyone like to go first?" If no one responds, venture an answer yourself and ask for comments.
- Model openness as you share with the group. Group members will follow your example. If you limit your sharing to a surface level, others will follow suit.
- Encourage multiple answers or responses before moving on.

- To help continue a discussion and give it greater depth, ask, "Why?" or "Why do you believe that?" or "Can you say more about that?"
- Affirm others' responses with comments such as "Great" or "Thanks" or "Good insight," especially if it's the first time someone has spoken during the group session.
- Monitor your own contributions. If you are doing most of the talking, back off so that you do not train the group to listen rather than speak up.
- Remember that you do not have all the answers. Your job is to keep the discussion going and encourage participation.

Managing the Session

- Honor the time schedule. If a session is running longer than expected, get consensus from the group before continuing beyond the agreed-upon ending time.
- Involve group members in various aspects of the group session, such as saying prayers or reading the Scripture.
- Note that the session guides sometimes call for breaking into smaller groups or pairs. This gives everyone a chance to speak and participate fully. Mix up the groups; don't let the same people pair up for every activity.
- As always in discussions that may involve personal sharing, confidentiality is essential. Group members should never pass along stories that have been shared in the group. Remind the group members at each session: confidentiality is crucial to the success of this study.

SESSION 1
JESUS RECONCILES

Planning the Session

Session Goals

As a result of conversations and activities connected with this session, group members should begin to

- respond to an Advent story about those on the graveyard shift;
- explore through Scripture how God calls the unsuspecting, the unqualified, and the undeserving;
- examine how our deepest longings for reconciliation are connected with God's desire to reconcile others;
- confront how our fears limit our response to God's call; and
- begin to explore how, where, and to whom group members believe they are sent.

Biblical Foundation

But the angel said to them, "Do not be afraid; for see—I am bringing you good news of great joy for all the people: to you is born this day in the city of David a Savior, who is the Messiah, the Lord." (Luke 2:10-11 NRSV)

Special Preparation

- If possible in advance of the first session, tell participants to bring either a notebook or an electronic means of journaling, such as a tablet. Provide writing paper and pens for those who may need them, as well as Bibles for those who did not bring one.
- On a large sheet of paper or a board, print and post the following statement: "Sometimes when you do something you don't normally do, you see something you don't normally see."
- Get an Advent wreath with four candles, as well as a lighter or matches (electronic candles are an alternative). Or if you prefer, simply place one candle on a table.
- If you decide to do the reenactment of Waffle House, set up a table with chairs on one side to serve as the counter of the restaurant. If your group is fairly small, this will be sufficient scenery. If you have twelve or more in the group, you may want to set up two or three smaller tables to act as booths.
- Prepare index cards with the following names: *Mary, shepherds, Zechariah, Elizabeth, Joseph.* Make multiple copies of each card so every participant can have one card.
- Post the following open-ended prompt: When I was terribly afraid and (longing for reconciliation, faced with a call, walking through the valley of the shadow of death), I experienced God's presence when . . .

- If you plan to use incense or a candle in the closing prayer, check to be sure that no one in the group is allergic or sensitive to strong fragrance.
- Get hymnals with "Silent Night! Holy Night!" and accompaniment for the hymn. If a piano or other instrument is not available, accompaniment can be found on the Internet.
- The closing prayer is a litany. You can photocopy the litany from page 23 and pass it out at before the closing prayer.
- Go over the session in advance and select or adapt the activities you think will work best for your group in the time allotted.

Getting Started

Opening Activity

As participants arrive, welcome them to the study. If group members are not familiar with one another, make nametags available. Provide Bibles for those who did not bring one.

Gather together, and invite group members to introduce themselves. Then call attention to the statement you posted. ("Sometimes when you do something you don't normally do, you see something you don't normally see.") Invite any volunteers who have had an experience like that to describe it and to tell what they saw. Discuss:

- If you've had such an experience, what was the result? Did you learn something new about yourself or someone else? Did you have a new insight?
- If you've never had an experience like this, why do you think this is true? Is it because you rarely do something outside your normal routine? Or is it perhaps because you are often too busy to see things from a new perspective?

Tell the group that in this session, they will hear a story of some people who departed from their normal routine and, as a result, found that it changed the way they viewed things.

Opening Prayer

Light one Advent candle. Pray the following or a prayer of your own choosing:

Come, Lord Jesus. Make us aware of your presence here with us today. As we have encountered you in the parables you told, open our hearts to new understandings through the stories we hear today. In your name we pray. Amen.

Learning Together

Video Study and Discussion

Introduce the group to Jorge Acevedo, lead author and host of the study and lead pastor at Grace Church, a multi-site United Methodist congregation in Southwest Florida. Grace Church is recognized as having one of the largest and most effective recovery ministries in America, with over seven hundred people involved in weekly recovery ministries. Participants can learn more about Acevedo and his church at their website, www.egracechurch.com.

To set the stage for the study, invite participants to think about how, where, and to whom they believe they are sent. Explain that this Advent study is story-based. Each week, a different presenter will tell a story about a memorable Advent or Christmas.

The first story is told by Jacob Armstrong, pastor of Providence United Methodist Church in Mt. Juliet, Tennessee. Ask participants to attend particularly to what Jacob's story has to do with those who work on the graveyard shift. Then watch the video. Following the viewing, discuss:

- In their conversation, Acevedo and his four coauthors discuss what it means to be in ministry to those on the third shift. What reasons do they give for people sometimes hesitating to minister to this group? How might we break those bounds and minister as Christ might have?
- How have you experienced both giving and receiving in your ministry as a disciple of Christ?

Bible and Book Study and Discussion

Roleplay the Third Shift

As a volunteer reads Luke 2:8-20, invite the group to listen for what the angels announced. In the book chapter, Jacob Armstrong points out how the angels use the word you in the announcement. Ask someone to read verses 10-11 again, emphasizing that word. Jacob suggests that the shepherds might have wondered why such a message was coming to them.

If they have not already done so, invite the group to read the short sections under the headings "Jesus Comes to the Unsuspecting," "Jesus Comes to the Unqualified," and "Jesus Comes to the Undeserving."

Recall that Jacob poses the following rhetorical question:

> If that grand announcement came tonight, would God go to Waffle House while it was still dark and tell the ladies who work all night?

Tell participants that they can participate in a roleplay of what might happen if the angels made their announcement at Waffle House. Ask for two or three volunteers to be the cooks and servers, and have them stand behind the "counter." Ask two or three others to agree to take the parts of those who have come in to eat at Waffle House—truck drivers, nurses, police officers, and so forth. Others could take similar roles and sit in the "booths," or simply stand by and observe.

Set the stage for the roleplay by saying something like the following:

> It's still dark in the early morning hours at Waffle House. The restaurant is empty at the moment, but soon the men and women who cook and serve food here will be hard at work—operating the grill, pouring coffee, taking orders, and clearing away the plates and cups.
>
> As usual, it's brightly lit inside the restaurant. And as usual, it's dark outside, except for the lights of cars and trucks on the highway. Suddenly, the darkness is illuminated by a blinding light that makes the restaurant lights seem dim. What could it be—an explosion, a fire, a UFO? Then the cooks and servers hear a voice: "Do not be afraid; for see—I am bringing you good news of great joy." The voice continues with unbelievable news, and then the sky is filled with heavenly creatures singing, "Glory to God! Go and see—then tell everyone."

Ask the volunteers to take up the story there, with the cooks and servers discussing what has just happened. Then have the other volunteers come in and take seats at the counter or in the booths, joining in the conversation.

Let the scene play out, then pause to debrief the roleplay, discussing some of the following:

Why do you think God would choose those on the graveyard shift to be first to hear the good news of the Messiah's birth?

- In what ways were the people in this roleplay unsuspecting, undeserving, and unqualified?
- To whom do you think the workers in Waffle House first would deliver their good news? To whom do you think the shepherds would first have delivered the news of the Messiah's birth?
- In his chapter, Jacob observes that God does not call the equipped, but equips the called. Have you experienced this in your life as a disciple? If so, how?

If you choose not to do the roleplay, simply have a discussion using some of the questions above.

Explore Our Longing and God's Longing

Form pairs. Point out that Jacob refers to the film *A Christmas Story*, where Ralphie longed for one special gift, a Red Ryder BB gun. Ask each person to think of one Christmas gift they can remember longing to receive. Have them tell their partner about that gift, answering the following:

- Why did you long for that gift? What did it represent? What was its appeal?
- Did you receive the gift? If so, did it meet your expectations?
- If you did not receive the gift, how did you feel?

Invite participants to follow along in their Bibles as a volunteer reads aloud Luke 1:5-25. Then ask the group to scan the information in the text about Zechariah and Elizabeth. Discuss:

Jacob invites us to imagine the people assembled just outside the Temple as Zechariah performed his priestly duties. What do you think the people were longing for?

Point out that, just as in the case of the message to the shepherds, the angel in this account had a personal message for Zechariah, telling him that *his* prayer had been heard. Discuss:

- What did Zechariah long for? How was the deepest longing of his heart connected to the longing of all the people of God?
- Jacob observes that often our deepest longings for reconciliation are connected to God's desire to reconcile others. What does he mean? Do you agree?

Explore Fear

Remind the group that in the video discussion, Rachel Billups names fear as one of the factors that make people hesitate to get involved in ministry. Jacob points out that the phrases "Fear not" and "Do not be afraid" are among the most commonly recurring phrases in Scripture. Discuss:

- People often experience fear when they realize God wants to use them. Why do you think this is so? Have you had that experience?

In the Advent narratives, it is not those who are bursting with courage and confidence whom God seems to use, but those who are utterly terrified to be included in the story. Distribute the character cards you prepared before the session. Have participants form one or more small groups of five, with each person in the group holding a different character card. Ask each person in a group to tell which character from the account of Jesus' birth they are holding and then to respond to the following open-ended prompt from the perspective of that character:

- When I received the angel's message, I was afraid because . . .

Wrapping Up

Closing Activities

Telling a Personal Story

Remind the group that in the introduction to the video, Jorge Acevedo asks:

- Do you have an Advent story? A story about Advent or Christmas that changed everything?

In the opening activity, you invited volunteers to tell a story about doing something they don't normally do, and as a result seeing something they don't normally see. Remind the group that in ending this chapter, Jacob tells of a time when he had a profound experience of Emmanuel—God with us—in a hospital waiting room. Call attention to the posted prompts: "When I was terribly afraid and (longing for reconciliation, faced with a call, walking through the valley of the shadow of death) I experienced God's presence when . . ." Then invite volunteers to describe their responses.

Being Reconciled, Being Sent

Call the group's attention to the following questions in the text:

- What are you longing for?
- Where do you need reconciliation?

Ask participants to read the paragraph following those questions silently, reflecting on the suggestions Jacob poses as possible answers to those questions. Invite adults to record in their journals their own personal answers to the questions of what is longed for and where they need reconciliation.

Jacob tells us that the promise of Advent is not just that God hears our longings and sends Jesus to reconcile us. God also sends us as messengers of that reconciliation. He ends this chapter by challenging us to consider where we are being sent and who else needs to be reconciled. Encourage adults to write in their journals personal answers to those questions.

If group members find that answers to those questions are elusive, ask them to jot down the questions for later reflection.

Also encourage them to read Chapter 2 in preparation for the next session.

Sing a Hymn

Sing together "Silent Night! Holy Night!"

Closing Prayer

Remind the group that in the account of Zechariah's experience in the Temple, the text tells us that the burning of incense was a way of symbolizing the prayers of God's people being lifted up to God. If you like, light incense or a scented candle.

Nowhere is it more evident that Jesus came for all people than in Luke's birth stories. Hand out the photocopies of the litany. Invite the group to join in the litany, with individuals or small groups reading the responses. (If your group is small, participants can read more than one response.)

A Litany of Affirmation and a Prayer of Expectation

Leader   *Jesus came for all people:*

Reader 1   *people whose expectations for their lives have changed;*

Reader 2   *who find themselves physically uncomfortable;*

Reader 3   *who drive crowded streets;*

Reader 4   *who feel like they live where they work;*

Reader 5   *who are afraid, even terrified;*

Reader 6   *who need good news;*

Reader 7   *who are in a hurry;*

Reader 8   *who are amazed by some things happening in their lives;*

Reader 9   *who are still processing some things happening in their lives.*

Leader   *Jesus was sent to a people in need, a people who were desperate for help—to people just like us.*

ALL   *Come, Lord Jesus. Send us—unsuspecting, unqualified, and undeserving as we are. In your holy name we pray. Amen.*

SESSION 2

JESUS SETS US FREE

Planning the Session

Session Goals

As a result of conversations and activities connected with this session, group members should begin to

- respond to an Advent story about someone who was able to see the divine in others;
- explore through Scripture Jesus' liberating mission and its implications for discipleship;
- examine how focusing on life circumstances can blind us to seeing the divine in others;
- recognize the many ways that they receive as well as give;
- use their gifts to express an understanding of how Jesus sets us free; and

- continue to explore how, where, and to whom they believe they are sent.

Biblical Foundation

Jesus went to Nazareth, where he had been raised. On the Sabbath he went to the synagogue as he normally did and stood up to read. The synagogue assistant gave him the scroll from the prophet Isaiah. He unrolled the scroll and found the place where it was written:

The Spirit of the Lord is upon me,
because the Lord has anointed me.
He has sent me to preach good news to the poor,
to proclaim release to the prisoners
and recovery of sight to the blind,
to liberate the oppressed,
and to proclaim the year of the Lord's favor.

(Luke 4:16-19 CEB)

Special Preparation

- In the center of a large sheet of paper, print the following: "Where do we need reconciliation in the world today?"
- Bring front sections of newspapers, or download and print information from Internet news sites.
- If possible, plan to show a YouTube clip of "Come, Thou Long-Expected Jesus." You will need a laptop and equipment for viewing the clip. You will also need hymnals that include the hymn, as well as accompaniment, for the closing.
- Again set up an Advent wreath, or place two candles on a table.

- On a large sheet of paper or a board, print the following: The purpose of Jesus' ministry, as he understood it, was to preach the gospel or good news to those whose life chances seem stifled economically, socially, physically, and/or mentally.
- Gather a variety of art materials: large drawing paper, markers or crayons, construction paper scraps, glue, tissue paper, and even recyclable materials.
- Remember that there are more activities than most groups will have time to complete. As leader, you'll want to go over the session in advance and select or adapt the activities you think will work best for your group in the time allotted.

Getting Started

Opening Activity

Welcome participants. When most have arrived, remind participants that the first chapter concluded with the suggestion that when they experience a deep longing at Christmas, they should think about reconciliation. Invite the group to look through the newspapers and downloads from Internet news sites and note headlines that point to pain, suffering, or a sense of hopelessness. Ask them to jot down these headlines on the large sheet of paper around the question. Ask group members to then read over the headlines in silence, reflecting on these recent examples of places where reconciliation is needed and bringing to mind other instances where pain, suffering, or hopelessness have been manifested over the past year.

Point out that the writer of this session, Lanecia Rouse, describes her routine for entering into the new Christian liturgical year. Although the group may be exploring this session in the second week of Advent, invite participants to join you in this ritual. Ask them to find a comfortable position for sitting and to breathe in deeply, then release their breath in a long exhale. Rouse observes that for her, this moment represents receiving the invitation Jesus extends when he says, "Come to me, all you who are struggling hard and carrying heavy loads, and I will give you rest" (Matthew 11:28 CEB). Invite the group to do as she suggests and spiritually breathe out all the pain, suffering, and hopelessness they have experienced in the year past and to prepare space to breathe in more of life with Christ.

Light two Advent candles. Show the video clip of the Advent hymn if you have it. As participants listen to the singers, invite them to reflect on the words in silence.

Opening Prayer

Come, Lord Jesus. As we await your coming anew at Christmas, we yearn for release from all our fears. Give us a sense of your liberating, challenging love. In your name we pray. Amen.

Learning Together

Video Study and Discussion

In the Session 2 video, we hear Lanecia Rouse tell the story of her friend Ms. Ruby and what happened on Christmas Eve when Ms. Ruby helped Lanecia host a group of men experiencing homelessness. Lanecia has ministered in both British Methodist and United Methodist churches, and in recent years she has served as project manager for The Art Project, Houston, a therapeutic art ministry for those experiencing homelessness. Invite the group to look for ways in which Ms. Ruby's "disability" could be termed a special ability to see people.

After viewing the video, invite the group to discuss some of the following:

- What do you think Ms. Ruby teaches us about seeing Jesus in other people?
- Lanecia speaks of how Ms. Ruby has made her more aware of her own "sight impairedness." What does she mean?
- What do you think are some reasons we miss seeing the divine in other people?
- In their discussion following the story, the writers speak of the sacrament of the present moment. How would you define it?
- How did Ms. Ruby help facilitate community among the men gathered for a meal and a place to sleep on Christmas Eve?

Bible and Book Study and Discussion

See Beyond Stifling Life Circumstances

Invite the group to follow along in their Bibles as a volunteer reads aloud Luke 4:16-19, this session's biblical foundation. Ask another volunteer to read aloud Isaiah 61:1-4, the passage Jesus was reading from the scroll. Call attention to the sentence you posted before the session and give them a chance to read and consider it. Point out that in her chapter, Lanecia Rouse observes that this is our mission as well: we are sent to offer empowering and enabling words to people who feel stifled in life by their circumstances. Invite the group to name as many people or groups of people as they can think of who they believe are living in stifling circumstances, and list these on the sheet of paper or the board.

Look together at how these persons or groups are named. Note that the writer speaks not of "the homeless" or "homeless people" but of persons "experiencing homelessness." Ask:

- What difference, if any, does it make in our perspective if we use "people first" language, as Lanecia does—that is, if we speak first of the person, then name the stifling life circumstance?
- Lanecia suggests that if we are able to live in the light of God's love and acceptance ourselves, we are better able to see the light of God in others and help them recognize it in themselves. Do you agree? When have you had this experience in sharing the good news?

Understanding Jesus' Call and Liberating Mission

Note for the group that while we are called to give the good news of God's liberating love to those who live in stifling circumstances, we often feel ill-equipped to do so. Form small groups or pairs and assign to each one of the following passages: Matthew 4:18-22; Matthew 9:9-10; Luke 8:1-3. Ask each pair or group to imagine being the human resources director for Jesus' ministry, charged with hiring disciples for him.

Using some of the following information, briefly describe what was involved in being a disciple of a rabbi such as Jesus:

> Both boys and girls began their study at age four or five in Beth Sefer (elementary school), held in conjunction with the local synagogue. Children memorized large portions of the Torah by the time they finished this level of education. At this point most students (and certainly the girls) stayed at home to help with the family, or in the case of boys to learn the family trade. The best students continued their

study in the secondary school, called the Beth Midrash, while learning a trade. Here they, along with the adults in the town, studied the prophets and the writings in addition to Torah and began to learn the interpretations of the Oral Torah. A small number of the most outstanding Beth Midrash students sought permission to study with a famous rabbi, often leaving home to travel with him for a lengthy period of time.

A person desiring to be the disciple would ask if he might "follow" the rabbi. The rabbi would then consider the student's potential to become like him, as well as his level of commitment. Most were probably turned away. (excerpted and adapted from the website *That the World May Know*, at https://www.thattheworldmayknow.com/rabbi-and-talmidim)

Ask pairs or groups to write a brief description of what the ideal candidate for discipleship with Jesus would bring to the enterprise. Then ask participants to read their assigned Scripture and write a brief assessment of how good a fit their candidate(s) would be for the position of disciple.

In the large group, have the smaller groups report. Discuss:

- In traditional first-century terms, how qualified were the people called by Jesus to be his disciples?

Invite volunteers to take the role of one of the disciples, such as Peter or John, and to describe reasons that person might have given for not responding to Jesus' call.

Call attention to what Lanecia labels as the long list of "buts" that she had when she was invited to respond to be project manager for The Art Project, Houston. Ask the group to imagine that they discern a call from God to become involved in some very challenging ministry.

It might be a call to professional church ministry, but it could also be an opportunity to make a vocational change, take on a job with the potential to make a difference, or agree to accept a volunteer role.

Ask the group to scan what Lanecia has to say about responding to God's call. In their journals, ask participants to make their own list of "buts" and possible responses.

Hear Stories of Responding to Unconditional Love

Point out to the group that in addition to the story of Ms. Ruby, Lanecia tells the stories of two other people whose lives were touched by The Art Project, Houston, and who in turn touched her life.

Form two groups. Assign to one group the story of the man in the shelter who participated in the jewelry-making workshop (under the heading "Jesus as Liberator") and to the other group the story of Sunshine (under the heading "Looking for Light"). Ask groups to read their stories silently and then discuss some of the following in their group:

- In this story, what seems to have been the empowering word or moment for the person experiencing homelessness?
- From this person, what did you learn about being homeless?
- In what ways do you see the light of God shining through this person's story?
- What do you identify as the gifts with which this person is endowed?
- How was Lanecia transformed by knowing this person? What is transforming for you in this story?

In the large group, invite each smaller group to report what surprises or insights they gleaned from the story they read and discussed.

Wrapping Up

Closing Activities

Create Images of Liberation

Remind the group that in her ministry with The Art Project, Houston, Lanecia experienced how people whose lives had been stunted by hopelessness were transformed by allowing the love of God to shine through and be refined in their lives. Her work has demonstrated the transformative power of using one's gifts.

Point participants to the art materials. Ask them to consider how Jesus sets us free to live lives empowered by God's love and transformed for ministry. Acknowledge that, for some people in the group, using art materials in creative ways may be intimidating. Encourage them to think of a way to use the materials in some way that best fits their gifts—for example, they might create visual images, but they might also use markers or crayons to combine words or phrases in interesting ways. Or they could list Scriptures, write a poem, copy hymns, or do whatever is the best fit for them in expressing what it means to be free.

After allowing time to work, invite participants to describe their creation. Display these in your space or in a location where they can be seen by others.

Tell a Personal Story

Recall for the group that in the story of Ms. Ruby, they encountered a person considered to have a disability, and yet she was able to discern the divine in other people. They also heard stories of people experiencing the hopelessness of being homeless and yet were liberated to the fuller life that God intends. Form pairs, and ask people to tell their partners of a similar experience of God's liberating love. If no such experience comes to mind, invite people to pray for their partners, giving thanks for the light of the divine evident in that person's life.

Suggest that adults consider one or more of the following in the coming week:

- Encourage adults to pray that their eyes be opened to the light of the divine that may be shining, whether dimly or brightly, in the lives of those they encounter.
- Suggest a simple spiritual exercise: Ask them to observe people they encounter in daily interactions whom they customarily may not notice: a grocery store clerk, people stocking shelves, people waiting at bus stops, and the like. Ask them to seek to discern God's light in those people and to offer a brief silent prayer for them.
- Adults might also want to use the simple breathing ritual from the opening activity for their devotions.

Also remind adults to read Chapter 3 of the book before the next session.

Sing a Hymn

Sing together "Come, Thou Long-Expected Jesus."

Closing Prayer

Come, Lord Jesus. Make us aware of your light shining in everyone we meet. Guide us as we seek to discern those people and places in need of restoration and newness of life, including ourselves. Give us insight into where you would have us go and what you would have us do as your disciples. Amen.

SESSION 3

JESUS IS GOD WITH US

Planning the Session

Session Goals

As a result of conversations and activities connected with this session, group members should begin to

- respond to a story of experiencing God's presence in the midst of an unexpected crisis;
- explore through Scripture the paradox of incarnation—God with us;
- examine how one experiences God with us in pain, in unknowing and fear, in waiting, and in joy; and
- continue to explore *how, where, and to whom they believe they are sent.*

Biblical Foundation

"The virgin will conceive and give birth to a son, and they will call him Immanuel" (which means "God with us").

(Matthew 1:23 NIV)

Special Preparation

- Justin LaRosa, the writer of this chapter, acknowledges that though his family's crisis experience ended well, for many others this is not the case. Be sensitive to the fact that there may be adults in your group whose crises have ended in tragedy, some of whom may be struggling with an understanding of where God was in that experience.
- On newsprint or a board, print the following questions: Can you remember a time when you were shocked unexpectedly to the core? How did you connect with or experience God before, during, and after?
- Again hang an Advent wreath, or simply set up three candles on a table.
- On one large sheet of paper, print *Jesus was fully human*. On another, print *Jesus was fully divine*.
- Head separate large sheets of paper each with one of the following: *pain, fear, waiting, joy*. Display at intervals around your space or on tabletops. Obtain self-stick notes and pens.
- Get hymnals with the carol "Hark! The Herald Angels Sing" and accompaniment for the carol.

Getting Started

Opening Activity

As participants arrive, welcome them. Call their attention to the posted questions. (Can you remember a time when you were shocked unexpectedly to the core? How did you connect with or experience God before, during, and after?) Form pairs, and invite each person to discuss the questions with their partner.

In the large group, invite volunteers to relate an experience they shared with their partner, as well as how they connected with God on that occasion. Discuss:

- What do you think helped you connect with God?

It may be that some people in the group have had traumatic experiences and were unable to sense God's presence in the midst of their experience. If so, invite them to think about the following:

- Why do you think you were unable to sense that God was with you in the midst of your pain? What do you think blocked you from connecting with God?
- Looking back, are you able to see that God was there with you, despite your pain? If not, why do you think this is so?

If there are volunteers willing to speak to these sensitive questions, invite them to do so.

Tell participants that in this session, they will hear the story of a family that was confronted with an unexpected crisis. Yet in the face of that experience, they were able to experience God's presence in the midst of their pain, fear, and uncertainty.

Opening Prayer

Light three Advent candles. Pray the following, or a prayer of your own choosing:

Come, Lord Jesus. In our pain and sorrow as well as in our joy, in life, and in death, when we feel your presence and when you seem far away, we know that we belong to you. Guide us as we seek to encounter you in Scripture and in our interactions with one another. Amen.

Learning Together

Video Study and Discussion

In the Session 3 video, we hear Justin LaRosa's story of a Christmas that changed everything for his family. Justin is a licensed clinical social worker. An ordained deacon, he previously served for eight years as director of discipleship for Hyde Park United Methodist Church in Tampa, Florida, and is now leading the downtown ministry and community gathering space at Hyde Park's second campus, The Portico. As participants view the video, invite them to find out how a phone call one Christmas changed Justin's perspective from excitement and anticipation to fear and uncertainty.

Following the video, discuss some of the following:

- In the video discussion, Jorge Acevedo observes that God whispers to us in our pleasure and shouts to us in our pain. Has this been your experience? If so, what happened?
- How did Justin LaRosa experience people to be the presence of God in this difficult time? What is a Zaky, and how did it signify God with us for the LaRosa family?
- In the discussion, Rachel Billups notes that the Advent season can be a very tough time for people who are experiencing pain and loneliness. She suggests that it should be a time for those in ministry to "lean in." What do you think she means by this? Do you think her suggestion applies only to those who are church professionals, or to all disciples?

- Lanecia Rouse speaks of having suffered a loss during one Advent and of experiencing people sitting with her on the mourner's bench. In such circumstances, how do you judge when words are needed and when simple presence is more helpful?
- Jacob Armstrong observes that often God inserts Godself into the busyness of our schedules. If you have experienced this, when and in what ways?

Bible and Book Study and Discussion

Explore Incarnation

Invite a volunteer to read aloud Matthew 1:18-25, the passage in which is today's foundational Scripture passage. Also ask someone to read aloud the second paragraph in the section "Meeting Us Where We Are," in which Justin mentions the Incarnation. Form two groups, and give each group one of the prepared large sheets of paper. Ask them to talk together about what it implies that Jesus was fully human or fully divine, and list all the implications.

In the large group, discuss:

- Why does Justin observe that the Incarnation, God with us, is a paradox?
- What does the Incarnation tell us about Jesus and the human experience?

Encounter God With Us in Pain

Remind the group that in Session 1 we explored what, in the birth story, Scriptures tell us about angels. We learned that angels are messengers. Justin observes that angels bring surprising news and alter the direction of people's lives.

Ask a volunteer to relate the significance of the angel pin and the role it played in Justin's story. Discuss:

- What surprising news did the angel bring to Zechariah? to Joseph? to Mary? to the shepherds? How did that news alter the direction of each person's life?
- What message do you think the angel pin delivered, and from whom did the message come?
- To Justin, how did the pin represent God with us?

Ask volunteers to summarize briefly Justin's description of the NICU (Neonatal Intensive Care Unit). Invite participants to describe similar places they have experienced—places where things are chaotic, messy, or challenging.

Encounter God in Unknowing and in Fear

Ask the group to think about a time when, like Justin, they were intensely afraid of what the future might hold. Ask them to name aloud the situation in a word or two. If people are willing, ask them to describe briefly what the circumstances were, how they were feeling, and what happened.

Have the group quickly scan the information about the blanket and The Zaky in the section "Jesus Is God With Us in Uncertainty and Fear." Invite participants with smartphones to view a Zaky online. Discuss:

- What did the blanket over Russell's incubator represent to Justin? Why?
- How was The Zaky a tangible reminder of God's love for Russell's parents?
- Have you ever experienced God's presence in a difficult time through a tangible object or a loving act extended to you by someone? If so, can you describe that experience?

Encounter God in Waiting

Remind participants that Advent is a time of waiting and preparation. Ask them to scan the information under the heading "Jesus Is God With Us in Waiting," in which Justin describes the sacred space where he prepared to see his son—the hospital chapel. Ask:

- Justin observes that silence helps us wait, but we must be willing to endure repetitive inner noise. How, if at all, does silence function for you in your faith life?

Invite the group to experience one way of cultivating inner stillness. Ask them to find a comfortable position for sitting and to breathe slowly and deeply, breathing out the distractions of the day and breathing in stillness and God's presence. Say that you will use Psalm 46:10 (NIV), "Be still, and know that I am God," as a way to move more deeply into silence. Encourage participants to continue breathing deeply and evenly as you repeat the line several times, interspersing the line with periods of silence. After a few minutes, debrief the experience with the group by asking their reactions. Discuss:

- Justin notes that some people are afraid of silence because they are afraid of what they may find there. What is your response to that idea?
- In this experience, what did you find distracting? difficult? freeing?

Tell the group that in the closing activities you'll be returning to some of the contemplative prayer practices Justin names.

Encounter God in Times of Joy

Invite someone to read aloud John 16:16-24. If anyone in the group has experienced childbirth, ask them to comment on the following:

- When Justin uses the metaphor of labor pains giving way to joy in holding the baby, does it ring true for you? If so, in what ways? If not, why?

Ask a volunteer to describe what happened in the bus station at the event called Carols in the City, in the section "Jesus Is God With Us in Times of Joy." Discuss:

- Can you name a time when you experienced joy unexpectedly, or when it was initiated by someone you least expected to communicate it, such as the man experiencing homelessness who was encountered by the caroling group?

Ask participants to form pairs, preferably with someone with whom they have not partnered before. Ask them to relate to one another a time when something painful ultimately gave way to an experience of joy. Be sensitive to the possibility that some people in the group may presently be going through difficult experiences, and in those cases invite their partners to pray for them, offering encouragement and hope, as Justin suggests.

Wrapping Up

Closing Activities

Examine Incarnational Signposts

In the chapter, Justin points out what he calls "incarnational signposts": an angel pin and a volunteer; a blanket and a knitter; a Zaky and a couple; silence and a waiting room; Carols in the City and a friend; a Christmas card and Russell. Justin suggests that in Advent we ourselves are challenged to be incarnational signposts to those who are in pain, in fear, are waiting, and have experienced joy.

Encourage participants to look in the coming week for people or incidents that seem to be incarnational signposts and for ways the participants might be incarnational signposts for others. Note that Justin's experience was the impetus for the NICU ministry initiated at his church. How might a person's similar painful experience spark a way to be sent to others?

Remind participants to read Chapter 4 in the text prior to the next session.

Sing a Hymn

Invite the group to sing "Hark! The Herald Angels Sing" as a reminder of the way angels brought surprising news to the people in the birth stories, and how the angels' news altered the directions of those people's lives. Also suggest that participants reflect on where they might encounter messengers from God who bring similar life-altering news.

Closing Prayer

Eternal God, we give thanks that Jesus was sent to be God-with-us. Give us new awareness of places in need of your incarnate love and of how we are sent to live out that love to a hurting world. Amen.

SESSION 4

JESUS BRINGS NEW LIFE

Planning the Session

Session Goals

As a result of conversations and activities connected with this session, group members should begin to

- respond to an Advent story about receiving an unexpected gift that was not wanted or welcome;
- examine evidence of dry bones in the church's life and consider where there might be signs of new life;
- explore, through Scripture, the power to speak new life over dry bones;
- consider the importance of connectedness and interrelatedness in bringing new life; and

- continue to explore how, where, and to whom they believe they are sent.

Biblical Foundation

The hand of the LORD was on me, and he brought me out by the Spirit of the LORD and set me in the middle of the valley; it was full of bones. . . . He asked me, "Son of man, can these bones live?" I said, "Sovereign LORD, you alone know." (Ezekiel 37:1, 3 NIV)

Special Preparation

- Continue to make available an Advent wreath, or simply set up four candles on a table.
- Wrap a large carton in Christmas gift wrap and tie with Christmas ribbon. Place on a table or on the floor in front of where participants will be seated.
- Obtain self-stick notes and pens.
- If you decide to present the Scripture as a dialogue between the prophet Ezekiel and God, recruit two readers in advance. Ask them to practice reading Ezekiel 37:1-14 so they can read their parts smoothly.
- On a large sheet of paper, print the following quote from Rachel Billups' colleague Mike Slaughter: "God does God's best work in cemeteries!"
- Obtain a picture of your church building and print the word *Closed* over it. If a photo is not available, simply make a sign with the name of your church, and print the word *Closed* over it in a contrasting color.
- On two large sheets of paper, sketch simple outlines of a body—such as you might for a very large paper doll or a gingerbread cookie cutter. Make the outlines cover most of the sheets.

- Obtain copies of a hymnal with the carol "In the Bleak Midwinter," and arrange for accompaniment.

Getting Started

Opening Activity

Welcome participants as they arrive. Remind them that in Session 1, they reflected on one Christmas gift that they longed for in the past. Point to the wrapped gift in front of them and ask:

- If you opened this Christmas gift and found inside the thing you most want for Christmas this year, what would it be?

Distribute self-stick notes and pens. Have participants jot down their answers on a note and attach it to the box. Read aloud some of the notes. Discuss:

- Which gifts are consumer goods we normally think of receiving as gifts—things such as an iPad, jewelry, clothing, cameras, sporting equipment, and the like?
- Who wrote down an intrinsic gift, such as the company of loved ones at a Christmas celebration, and what was it?
- Which of the gifts are things you actually need, and which are merely things you want?

Tell participants that in this session, they will hear about how an unexpected and unwanted gift opened one pastor's eyes to a new vision for her congregation.

Opening Prayer

Light four Advent candles. Pray the following, or a prayer of your choosing:

Come, Lord Jesus. Amid the glitter of the shopping season, we long for another kind of gift—the time to anticipate your coming anew at Christmas. By your Spirit and through your Word, come and fill our hearts with your peace. Amen.

Learning Together

Video Study and Discussion

In the Session 4 video, Rachel Billups tells of receiving a gift she hadn't expected and didn't really want. Rachel is the executive pastor of discipleship and part of the preaching team at Ginghamsburg Church in Tipp City, Ohio. Previously Rachel, an ordained elder in The United Methodist Church, served as the lead pastor of Shiloh United Methodist, a multi-site church in Cincinnati, Ohio. Before viewing the video, ask participants to watch for how a Christmas tree skirt could become a symbol of new life.

Following the video, discuss some of the following:

- Rachel Billups observes that sometimes pastors can delude themselves into thinking they have all the right answers. Why didn't the unexpected gift of a hand-knitted Christmas tree skirt fit into her box?
- Consider this question posed to the group by Jorge Acevedo: How have you found Jesus bringing you unexpected gifts?
- Justin LaRosa remarks that sometimes anger can precede new life. What does he mean? Have you experienced this?
- Lanecia Rouse points out that no one expected a Messiah to come in the form of an infant. What has she learned about goodness and love on the margins of society?

- Rachel speaks of how in the church we want access to the best and most abundant resources for our ministries, yet we often fail to see that what we actually have available is the best gift. What is that gift, and why is it so important?

Bible and Book Study and Discussion

Explore the Image of Dry Bones

Tell participants that the Scripture for this session comes from one of the Old Testament prophets, but not a prophet we customarily read during Advent. Instead, the Scripture is a passage from Ezekiel that recounts the prophet's vision of dry bones. Review what Rachel says about the context of the passage. Then invite the group to close their eyes and allow themselves to imagine the scene in their mind's eye. If you recruited two readers, have them read Ezekiel 37:1-14 as a dialogue. Otherwise, read it aloud yourself. Discuss:

- Describe the scene you imagined.
- Rachel sees scenes of genocides in this image. What comes to mind for you?

Ask the group to review briefly the information under the heading "Dry Bones." Invite them to name statistics the writer includes, as well as other indications that point to a church that may appear to be a pile of dry bones. Look together at the sign you posted prior to class showing your church with the word *Closed* plastered over it. Discuss:

- What is your sense of the general health of the larger church?
- How healthy and vibrant would you say your particular congregation is? If you closed your doors permanently tomorrow, do you think your community would miss it? Why, or why not?

Invite someone to read Ezekiel 37:3-6 aloud again. Call attention
to the sign you posted prior to class with a quotation from Rachel's
colleague Mike Slaughter. Rachel observes that, far from being a
vision of dry bones, Ezekiel actually has painted a picture ripe with
possibilities for new life. Form pairs or small groups. Invite each group
to consider the following:

- Where in your life as a congregation do you see evidence of
  dry bones?
- Where do you see signs that God is at work bringing new life
  or showing potential for new life?

After allowing a few minutes for groups to work, invite each to report.
Record the evidence of "dry bones" on one board or a large sheet of
paper, and the signs of new life on another.

Explore the Power of Words

Remind the group that in Scripture, the Word is a source of power:
by God's word creation came into being. John speaks of Jesus as the
Word made flesh. Rachel observes that our words also have power,
and she cites the example of some words that indicate a lack of vision.

Invite the group to name other words or phrases they may have
heard spoken in the church parking lot, in online posts, or in casual
conversation that indicate a lack of vision, or a vision of dry bones.
Then ask them to think of words of encouragement that point to
new life, for a church whose vision is limited or for persons who feel
hopeless or discouraged. Discuss:

- Rachel poses the question: What would happen if we,
  like Ezekiel, began speaking prophetic and encouraging
  words over ourselves? What examples does she give of what
  happened at Duke's Chapel Church?

- Do you hear the rattling sound of dry bones in your life as a congregation? Where and how is it manifesting itself?
- In the valley of dry bones, what gave life to the tendons and flesh and skin of the reconstituted bodies? What can we learn from this metaphor?

Consider Metaphors of Connectedness

Remind the group that in the New Testament, there is another passage that uses the human body as a metaphor, this time for the church. Form two groups and give each group one of the sheets of paper with body outlines, along with markers. Assign to one group Ezekiel 37:1-14 and to the other group 1 Corinthians 12:12-31.

Ask the groups to read their Scriptures, discuss the implications of the metaphor, and jot down their observations on the sheets of paper, in and around the outlines of a human body. In the large group, have each smaller group present a summary of their discussion using the body outline to illustrate it. Remind them of the old song "Dem Bones," in which the song brings the bones together using the word *connected*: the toe bone connected to the foot bone, and so on. Then discuss:

- What do the metaphors in "Dem Bones" say about the significance of being connected?
- What gives life to the body? What is the importance of gifts to the body?
- Do bones and sinews, a foot or an eye, function well alone? What does your answer say about our interconnectedness in the body of Christ?
- If we extend the metaphor, what is the implication for using our gifts to bring new life to the church? to our individual lives as Christians?

51

Wrapping Up

Closing Activities

Reflect on a Personal Story

In the video discussion, Jorge Acevedo speaks of having in his office a number of gifts he has been given by members of his congregation. While many of these gifts have monetary or artistic value, there are other gifts that on the surface may appear to be laughable, quirky, or so modest that they hardly seem worth giving. Yet sometimes these are the very gifts that carry the most value.

Ask participants to focus their attention again on the gift you wrapped before the session, and to imagine that inside the box is a gift that they—like Donna, the tree skirt knitter—have to offer the church. Invite them to reflect on the following:

- How might your gift to the church, though it may seem quite modest, bring new life?
- In what ways might your gift represent God's call—a way to be the hands and feet of Christ—in your community and in the world?

Suggest that adults consider one or more of the following in the coming week:

- As they engage in Bible study during the coming week, ask them to think about what their gifts are and how God might be calling them to use those gifts for the encouragement and affirmation of others, as well as for the furthering of God's mission in the world. Remind them that the gifts Donna offered to God through Duke's Chapel Church may have seemed modest and commonplace, but God's Spirit was able to use those gifts to breathe new life into the church. Encourage them to list their gifts in their journals.

- Rachel notes that Advent is the perfect time to open ourselves to the indwelling of God's spirit, breathing new life into each of us. Invite the group to sing the hymn "Spirit of the Living God" as a part of their devotional time.

Encourage participants to read book Chapter 5 during the coming week, the week before Christmas. This study can be done over four or five weeks, depending on whether your group wants a fifth session during Christmas week. If your group is doing a four-week study, Chapter 5 will serve as an epilogue. If your group is doing a five-week study, Chapter 5 will be the basis for the following week's session.

Sing a Hymn

Remind the group that in offering our gifts to God and accepting God's call to use our gifts, we are offering the best gift of all—the commitment to God of all that we are. Sing the last stanza of the Christmas carol "In the Bleak Midwinter," or read it aloud together.

Closing Prayer

Loving God, we give thanks for the gift of Jesus Christ. By your Spirit, help us to discern where, when, and by whom our gifts are needed, and stir us to a wholehearted offering of those gifts in your name. Amen.

SESSION 5 (OPTIONAL)
JESUS CHANGES EVERYTHING

Planning the Session

Session Goals

As a result of conversations and activities connected with this session, group members should begin to

- respond to an Advent story about a dream;
- discover, through Scripture, why Jesus came in the fullness of time;
- explore, through Scripture, the significance of grace and truth in Jesus' identity and our relationship with him;
- revisit why Jesus was sent to reconcile, to set us free, to be God with us, to bring new life, and to change everything;
- affirm and celebrate new understandings of why, where, and to whom we are sent; and
- recommit to God's call to be sent.

Biblical Foundation

When the right time came, God sent his Son, born of a woman . . .
(Galatians 4:4a NLT)

Special Preparation

- On a large sheet of paper or a board, print the following:
  What are the odds?
- If you are using this session following Christmas Day, set up
  one white candle on a table. If it is still the season of Advent,
  light the appropriate number of Advent candles.
- If you think no one will have access to a smartphone, go
  to Biblegateway.com and print Galatians 4:4a in several
  translations, or obtain copies of Bibles in several translations,
  including at least one copy of the NRSV Bible.
- On each of four large sheets of paper, print one of the first
  four chapter titles for the book *Sent*: "Jesus Reconciles,"
  "Jesus Sets Us Free," "Jesus Is God With Us," and "Jesus
  Brings New Life."
- Have available Bibles, writing paper, and pens for those who
  did not bring them.
- Obtain hymnals and choose a hymn of commitment for the
  closing, such as "Sent Out in Jesus' Name," "Take My Life
  and Let It Be," or "Send Me, Jesus" ("Thuma Mina"). Arrange
  for accompaniment, or recite the lines together.

Getting Started

Opening Activity

Welcome participants to this final session. Point out the question
you posted. (What are the odds?) Invite the group to review

Jorge Acevedo's story and jot down statements or statistics that they think are particularly relevant.

Form pairs, in which participants describe how their parents met. Were any details surprising or seemingly coincidental? Without actually doing any mathematical calculations, what do you think the odds might have been that those two people would get together?

In the large group, ask volunteers to respond to the following open-ended prompt: If it hadn't been for _____, my parents might never have met, and I might not have been born.

Tell the group that in this final session, they will find affirmation, not only that each person is a miracle but that, in response to Jesus' call, they should go forth and act like the miracles they are.

Opening Prayer

Light one candle to represent the coming of Jesus into the world at Christmas (or the appropriate number of Advent candles). Pray the following or a prayer of your choosing:

Loving God, we give thanks for the coming of Jesus Christ, the Word made flesh, who came to dwell among us, full of grace and truth. Speak to us now through your Scriptures. Through your Son, shine on us the light of your love. Amen.

Learning Together

Video Study and Discussion

In video Session 5, Jorge Acevedo describes a dream that prompted him to do a Google search. As we learned in Session 1, Acevedo is lead pastor at Grace Church, a multi-site United Methodist congregation in Southwest Florida. Grace Church is recognized as having one of the largest and most effective recovery ministries in America with over seven hundred people involved in weekly recovery ministries.

To set the stage for watching the video segment, invite participants to listen for evidence and statistics cited by blogger Ali Binazir. Following the segment, discuss some of the following:

- According to Jorge, what does God's miracle prove about each of us? What should be our response?
- Rachel Billups speaks of "holy hoarding." What do you think it is, and how does God respond?
- When Lanecia Rouse mentions the "feeding of the five thousand" as a favorite Bible passage, Acevedo points out something about Jesus' actions in that story that he had not previously noticed. What is it?
- What does Acevedo say is Jesus' favorite word? What are the implications for us?

Bible and Book Study and Discussion

Discover the Right Timing

Ask a volunteer to read aloud Galatians 4:4a. Using multiple translations or the website BibleGateway.com, encourage the group to listen to various ways the words "when the fulfillment of the time came" are translated.

On a large sheet of paper, print the words "In the fullness of time," "When the time was just right," or whatever phrase is used in the Bible translation most adults have. Ask participants to review the section "Jesus Changed Everything in the World" and discuss:

- What evidence does Jorge give for the argument that Jesus came in the fullness of time?
- He contends that Jesus' birth during the time of Herod made it just the right time. Why? Would you agree? If you had to choose a contemporary metaphor for evil comparable to Herod, what would you choose?
- Jorge observes that Jesus' birth was not just right on time; it was also on purpose. He says that Jesus changed everything on the planet. Would you agree? Why, or why not?

Explore Grace and Truth

Invite a volunteer to read aloud the passage from John 1 included in the book. Ask someone else to read the same passage from an NRSV Bible. Point out that "unfailing love and faithfulness" in one translation is "full of grace and truth" in another.

- What does Jorge mean when he says that God's grace will wreck your life and you'll love it?
- Why does Jorge say it's so important for believers that Jesus is full of both grace and truth?

Wrapping Up

Closing Activities

Revisit Being Sent

Form four smaller groups, and assign to each group one of first four book chapters. Give each group the large sheet of paper with the corresponding chapter title that you prepared before the session.

In each group, ask participants to briefly review their chapter, summarizing the story told by the writer and discussing insights they remember, questions they may still have, and anything that particularly struck them about being sent to be Christ's hands and feet in the world. Ask them to use their sheet to record key words and phrases from the discussion.

After allowing the smaller groups several minutes to work, have each group report to the large group. Invite participants to make their own observations about each chapter.

Point out that in the conclusion of Chapter 5, Jorge recounts how he preached on Christmas Eve while holding his friends' new baby. Invite participants to imagine a newborn child, in contrast to the culture of our planet, where power, prominence, prestige, and profits prevail. Encourage them to consider how we might be messengers of the good news, even as a baby brought good news on that first Christmas.

Sing a Hymn

Tell the group that although Christmas carols might seem more appropriate, it is fitting to conclude this study by singing a hymn of commitment. Sing or recite together the hymn you chose during preparation for this session.

Closing Prayer

Use a bidding prayer to close the study. Inform participants that there were will be pauses during which they can name aloud or pray silently for places in need of reconciliation.

Leader   *Gracious and loving God, we give thanks for the gift of Jesus Christ, whose coming into the world we celebrate again this day.*

We give thanks that Jesus came to reconcile, to restore the wholeness we yearn for, both for ourselves and for

the hurting world. Today we pray for reconciliation
in all these places:

(Allow time for participants to name places in need of reconciliation,
both aloud and in the silence of their hearts.)

We give thanks that Jesus came to set us free from
systems that impoverish and stunt, from the bondage
of addictions and diminished opportunities, and from
our own sinful natures. Today we pray for freedom in
all these places:

(Allow time for participants to name places in need of reconciliation,
both aloud and in the silence of their hearts.)

We give thanks that Jesus is God with us. We give
thanks for your presence in our pain and alienation,
in our sorrow and grief, in facing overwhelming
obstacles and places of hopelessness. Today we pray
for your abiding presence in all these places:

(Allow time for participants to name places in need of reconciliation,
both aloud and in the silence of their hearts.)

We give thanks that you bring us new life, in the midst
of barrenness and stunted possibilities, in alienation
and despair, even in the face of death. Today we pray
for your evidence of new life in all these places:

(Allow time for participants to name places in need of reconciliation,
both aloud and in the silence of their hearts.)

Just as you sent Jesus, help us to be your hands and feet,
delivering the gift of hope to a world in need. In the
name of Jesus Christ, whom you sent and by whom we
are sent into the world. Amen.

CPSIA information can be obtained at www.ICGtesting.com
Printed in the USA
LVOW07s0709221015

459206LV00001B/1/P